Bricks and Ballads

ALISON BRACKENBURY was born in Lincolnshire in 1953. She was educated at St Hugh's College, Oxford, and now lives in Gloucestershire and works in the family metal-finishing business. Her previous publications with Carcanet include *Dreams of Power* (1981), *Breaking Ground* (1984), *Christmas Roses* (1988), *1829* (1995), which was produced on BBC Radio 3, and *After Beethoven* (2000). Her *Selected Poems* were brought out by Carcanet in 1991. Her work recently won a Cholmondeley award.

ALISON BRACKENBURY

Bricks and Ballads

CARCANET

Acknowledgements

Alison Brackenbury's website (www.alisonbrackenbury.co.uk), *Boomerang* (www.boomerang.com), *Critical Quarterly*, *Leviathan*, *Magma*, *Metre*, *PN Review*, *Poetry London*, *Poetry Review*, *Smith's Knoll*, *Snakeskin* (homepages.nildram.co.uk), *Tabla*, *The Reader*, *The Rialto*, *The Times Literary Supplement*, *Thumbscrew*.

'Epigrams' was included in the anthology *101 Poems to Keep You Sane*, edited by Daisy Goodwin, HarperCollins, 2001.

'Tabby', 'At Home', 'The Story of Sigurd', 'The Blue Door', 'After the Rats', 'What' and 'The Lincolnshire Accent' were included in *The Story of Sigurd*, a limited fine press edition published by the Gruffyground Press in 2002.

First published in Great Britain in 2004 by
Carcanet Press Limited
Alliance House
Cross Street
Manchester M2 7AQ

A CIP catalogue record for this book is available from the British Library
ISBN 1 85754 751 9

The publisher acknowledges financial assistance from Arts Council England

Typeset in Bembo by XL Publishing Services
Printed and bound in England by SRP Ltd, Exeter

Contents

At the Beginning

It was the time of bombs or rumours of them
When ash from burnt towers fell upon the lips
Like an unanswered prayer. From your great height
You know what we did then

Whether we fought long wars, so young men died
In the cold passes; if the solid shops,
Bus stations, rose in dust; if our great planes
Blazed on the mountainside.

Trust me, it was a time when we would start
At dusked skin of a wrist, at a plane's drone.
I could predict, unsleeping, their success.
The war was theirs. The terror was our own.

Epigrams

My Latin has left me,
which may be as well.
They were brute engineers
and their afterlife, hell.

Only one tag stays:
a bird with no wings.
'In medias res'
in the middle of things.

I am weighed down by parents,
made mad by my child.
The late sky is sleeting
the garden is wild.

I slump on a chair
in the last glow day brings.
In medias res
in the muddle of things.

Self-set

It is the wild cranesbill
Seed stolen from the hedge.
It opens mouths of warm blue
White whispers at its edge.

As in this strange wet summer
The sodden, tame rose lists
It glimmers light. As rain itself
It stubbornly persists.

It is the wild cranesbill.
The lost are gone with you.
It neither owns nor saves us.
Its cups glow clearest blue.

The Blue Door

The door swings slowly to one side.
As people cough before the play
A rectangle of blue light rides

Behind the stage. There's nothing there
But dust and cold, the little comb
Which slipped from the last dancer's hair

Which she will never see again:
The glow on dunes the child saw,
Sea's plain beyond, then the sky's pane

Above the lover's bed, the cry
Of day reflected back again:
A blue square in the baby's eye.

The light grows richer, stills then thins.
The dark is quiet. The play begins.

The Sonnets

I planned to take these lines apart,
The story lies too close to lose.
The young man's fingers grip his heart.

Each betrays each. The woman comes.
Both sleep with her. How do they part?
He buys the grandest house in town

Where his wife stays. The boy moves on.
Thick body creaking, he retires.
Only once, toils back to London,

Climbs to lawyers; on the landing
The short breaths stop. The faintness flares.
He leans against the greasy wall.
Their laugh breaks round him, down the stairs.

On the Second of August

Oh I am very tired, but the old horse is dead
I had for eighteen years.
He was twenty-eight. Do you like horses?
One day you will be dead.

His coat shone red; the tumour in his eye
also flared red.
He lowered his head kindly.

You will not be shot, as the old horse was shot,
at nine o'clock in the wheat field
as the light wind drew from the south
as the light rain rustled hay
and he died with corn in his mouth.

Calf Sound

You heard the seal upon its rock
Neither fish nor deer
Black and glossy, silk of sea
Its cry rose clear

A lilting voice, a keening
The wind ran in that call
The white song that a bone blew
The love in it would kill.

You will not be a kind mother
Or faithful to your kin
If you stay on the cropped green turf.
Come in. Come in.

The hut has clouded windows
Kettles, dry plates, strong tea.
Your black eyes swim with moon's light
The dripping track to sea.

Heatwave

There are strawberries in the fields
Girls are wearing almost nothing
The washing blows in fragrant folds
Neighbours of the endless evening
Spray watermists, calling, chatting.

I am out, in the dipping grass,
My worn skin glows brown through my sleeve,
The burnished clouds glitter and pass.
As late birds, the tired children leave,
Gold fills my throat. I cannot breathe.

Mithras and the Milkman

Mithras Lord of the Sun has killed the bull,
The soldiers praise him.
In the North-East he stopped the wall of wind.
Upon Thames' banks he carved the muddy cave.
The soldiers praised him

Who stole him from the Persians. On the way
His red-hot birth was dulled to Christmas Day.

On Boxing Day the milkman sails through dark.
Whine of the motor cuts inside his head.
He lost his wife, a son and several teeth,
My note 'Two, please'. Three pints crash down instead.
I wake in sweat, wrestle through tangled sheets.
He climbs the cab's hot cave. The bull is dead.

Flight

It was bright and fat
As it fluttered the grass.
Cat rattled the fence, rushed
Its spilt sun, the brass

Of its light voice; as I ran
My cloth flapped. It flew.
Hail raked through the gardens.
The sky burned steel-blue.

All day I think of it
While at Europe's edge
The refugees pause.
Child sleeps by a hedge.

So in a third country
Whose words will not rhyme
By a warm foreign body
Far out of my time

Someone thinks of a room
The cage they left; still
The canary bursts dark
With its bubble and trill.

Forecasts

They say it is going to snow. I have been out rescuing roses.
It is not their fault that we heated the world, they flowered
On December the twenty-fourth. They are out in the dark.
The cat runs after me, squeaking. Lightly scratched
I lift them, uncoloured by streetlights. I search round the back,
Fall over stones, into half-flooded grass, then the cat.
My daughter is on the phone, to the latest boy,
Sprawled by the fire. 'My mother's been out in the dark –
Do you call those flowers?' They are sodden and battered.
One petal hangs brown; but under my nose
Lifts their warm earnest scent. I forage wet night
For leaves; the spiked curry-plant, throbbing air's water
Silver on silver; lamium, snake-flower,
Whose tongues of leaf smudge confiding white.
As fingers thaw, my daughter falls quiet, I remember
The unfurled primroses, glistening. I must go back out in the dark.

At Home

Mr Handel's friend comes to dinner.
They dine upon ordinary fare.
Handel slips into a sideroom.
His friend creeps up on him there.

He guzzles the finest claret.
He rips a chicken's white breast.
In a bare room lit by mirrors
Handel forgets his guest.

Scratching down music will blind him.
Enormous, lonely and odd,
In the clouded gilt of his mirror
George Handel nods to God.

Relics

I have come to see the angel
With her worn stone nose.
She came from the old church.
No one knows

Why it burnt down.
Knocked candle? Cromwell's men?
Victorian vestries
Raised her into rain.

I have no right to come here.
Their God and I are strangers.
They pinned her to an inner wall
Out of the weather's dangers

Out of the wind of lime-flower
Out of the sunlight's tide.
I drink her gaze, then leave her.
She hobbles at my side.

Blackthorn Winter

Late rain drove them all from the stableyard.
Gina's old thoroughbred, stiff in blue rugs,
Carla's iron-grey Carmen (who whinnies, tugs,
Though only waist-high) snatched hay, then stared.
While jeeps, a battered van beat a retreat,
The pony trotted me through the dusk's sleet.

Tender white glow on the circle of hills
Whirled into snow, soaked the mud from my sleeves,
Darkened the tips of the pony's small ears.
We galloped down tracks. No sight of a bird
Or living soul met us. Icy mud blurred
Into our faces. The feeble bulb spilled

Green on the hay I crammed into her rack
From the storm of the dark. Everything fell
In the unseen mud, key, gloves, soaked towel.
Then strange windows glimmered behind my back,
My car: furred snow-soft. No stars filled the dead
Eye of the sky, blind with flake. I, too, fled.

It skimmed the slope where small houses once lay,
The first, lost village. As swift as the snow
It was a hare. It was vast. It dropped low
Into feathers of white. The great ears reared,
It bounded out of my beam, then careered
To hedge-holes, brambles, to wait for wet day.

How long is an evening? Who would have thought
After all this, that a main traffic light
Would freeze on red; so I had to swing right
In the small town, where the snow had now thawed
To a sharp iced rain, to wander the grounds
Of dark, new bungalows, where I turned round.

Lost in a courtyard, I wrenched the wheel right.
Behind warm windows from ceiling to floor
Hunched and alert, the men watched me. I saw
One spin a wheelchair. Under their glass
Sheltered from mud and ice, soaring but fast,
White hyacinths opened into the made light.

Tess

I hate the book, except the end
In which the lovers break
Into an empty house and lie
In dust and warmth and ache

Inside the endless minutes.
The clothes sleep on the floor.
The soft old woman sent to clean
In silence shuts the door.

She is half-deaf and yet she hears
Men tramp with steady feet.
The rider thuds the clearing's shade.
The black cars block the street.

Homework. Write a Sonnet. About Love?

There are too many sonnets about love.
First let us name, then freeze, their eager faults.
(Who is it whistles, piercingly, above?
By the dark fields, the engine shudders, halts.)
No lover ever worried about fame,
More than the pearls, which tumbled round her ears.
(It might be Russia, when the quick thaw came;
Down steel steps, with a bundle, she appears.)
Nor were they ever read without a yawn;
The one who longed for them received no word.
(Behind her fall the lights of the low town.
She leaves the tracks. She whistles like a bird.)
The sonnet has no room to make an end,
The poplars dance. She takes the sudden bend.

Holiday

Christmas. I go back to bed with a fig
Whose belly is plump and swollen with seeds,
Crisp, gold as small fires, yet in each one
Is something dark and thick, which needs
To linger and be kept with care.
For the days are short, then the mornings start
Darker, as we freeze and work.
Earth fills the seeds at the lost fig's heart.

Put Down

We do not plan when people are to die
Habitually. With horses, it must be
Considered. The old horse's streaming eye
Betrays a tumour. Though he calls for mints
Bangs a broad hoof for dinner on the door,
Swerves headlong through wet grass, one day, the lid
Will close upon an eye lit blue as rain,
The past. The future, says the vet, is pain.

He must not go by box. He hates to ride,
So Bristol is too far. It must be home.
He will step out, black-stockinged, the three strides
Outside his door, stand calmly to be shot.
I will not give him to the hated Hunt.
But he will be a carcass. It does not
Matter if the petman comes, for that
(Not duck or calf) will feed a glossy cat.

For I am not my body, but the breath
The Greeks called soul, which blows away from lips,
Leaves us a gramme's shake lighter after death.
I will not spoil six paces of good earth
Unless I feed a tree. Rough ashes may
Blow anywhere, wear down to useful dirt.
But I will not be there, by plan or luck,
When warm bay flanks swing hoisted on their truck.

Greenfinch

It is pale and neat as a leaf
In half-dark, the star-dark, beneath

The whitethorn, blackthorn. Loll of head,
Stillness to hand's heat sing out dead.

Its breathy whistle fluttered, spun.
The cat heard. All those light lives, gone.

I shift it, swiftly. Do not cry,
See seven finches swoop from sky.

Out Walking

I met her in the beechwood.
The blood was on her paws.
In a blue gap of frostlight
She licked, then gnawed her claws.

'Why do you look so startled?'
'This is an English wood.
Your eyes are drowsy with warm seas.
Are the proud dead your food?'

'The frost is my equator.
The trenched field is my street.
In fur-lined cloak or leather
I smile on all I meet.'

'Why does that black fur melt?
Why does your white skin glow?'
'This time you would not touch –
Next time you will not know.'

Transported

I follow the supermarket lorry
With bread and apples, rosy lychees.
It is long as my house, its sides, white cliffs.
Twice the height of the beasts my father drove,
It soars by low hedges. How my heart lifts

At the sweep and snow of these great lorries
At their settled roar, their miles of power.
Though they wake the dead with the shake of steel
Though they block our lungs, then this narrow road
While the driver swears at his sun-baked wheel.

Before the Hay

This is the grass which hides the weed,
Ragwort, for which we trudge to look:
Grass whose plumes make lakes of jeans,
Grass which made the pony lame,
Threatened her life with poisoned blood,
Grass whose stems kiss on our graves.

The child I thought would trail and whine;
Raised dripping in her mother's arms
Says dreamily, 'The colours shine,
See the colours!' Nod and pass
Silvered purples, sighed greens, soft creams.
These are our flowers. This is the grass.

Tabby

You played upon the driveway,
You tapped the leaves' dry skin
Your brother blocked the cat flap
To stop you bounding in.

I finished with the paper,
Its cartoons and its cares.
I walked in the bright hallway.
You sat upon the stairs.

How had you crossed the kitchen?
When had the flap slammed flat?
You stared at me unblinking.
Death is a quiet cat.

The Card

Divorce comes close to death. I knew them at sixteen.
They sent each other Mars Bars through the post
Which the sorting rollers crushed. I think the priest
Who married them is dead; but he died young.
How she laughed before her wedding, deep-throated in the porch.

Houses grew bigger, and their elder son
Mounted disaster; but for thirty years
Their garden filled with butterflies, and cake
On rocking tables. Last time, her black bitch
Nervous from rescue, tailed her everywhere.
Its sheepdog's eyes shone rimmed with brilliant white.

I ought to cut our grass, but cannot think.
I sink upon the stairs as in a fog,
I hunt for the address. 'Is autumn free?
I'll see you then. I'm fine. I kept the dog.'

Dealer

They had to push the stretcher through the window.
He had filled the house with books, and jugs,
Decanters; teapots. At the end
He would choke his car with catalogues
In the auctions' dusk. 'R. Summerfield,
Dealer', peeled the paint above his door.
Pale as the paint he stood, jingled thin change,
Blocked the low doorway, daring you to buy.
Yet I bought two lots from him, both jugs,
One brought back from his house, before he closed.
Tawny on blue, they burn. He had the eye.

No one saw – for what was there to see? –
At the grand launch of the refurbished house,
The luxury apartments builders made
After Ron's messy end. Why did she sag
Out of the lineup? Only a woman, faint.
By blank, pale walls, the ruffled curtains' fall,
She whispered to the builder, 'Something pushed me.'
His tan went white. 'That's where we bricked the door.'

Beyond the canapés, beyond the noise,
First dusts glinted; fell quieter than a mouse.
Ron, stacked with unread books, three perfect jugs,
Pushed through the ghosts to fill his empty house.

Say

There is another world
A warm place in the head
Where thoughts stand stacked like cards.
Say, if my love were dead

Where would I go? To him,
The dour house on the hill,
(She would have left by then)
Boots on the step, plates still

Amongst the half-plucked birds
Float in the sink's grease tide.
Past shooting calendars
His field's floods shine and slide.

He never meant to farm.
He was dragged out of school
Drudged in wet yards, hot cabs.
He drowsed, as the plough's pull

Splintered a hated hedge;
Read history at night.
Come to the theatre,
Whose trembling line of light

Widens the curtained stage.
'It's something quite obscure.
The treatments wear him out.'
The blunt friends shrug. 'No cure.'

Is there another world?
His fields fill evening's trance.
Swifts sweep the hot, steep roof.
His shadowed curtains dance.

What

What will you see when you walk past my garden?
The delicate cowslip which scatters through stones
Soft whirls of leaf which the frosts cannot harden,
Or scyllas, the small stars which Turkey's rocks bred
Seen first through the fogs, a flash of blue light,
Wild honesty, which takes two years to flower
Then drifts from true purple to strange flecks of white.

By the fence crowds the whitethorn, fruiting to sloes.
Though the bullfinches hack at its windy height
Its flowers grow thick then drift into late snow.
The rowan will stink, cream as meadowsweet.
Old roses too heavy for posts they swarm on
Cloud over your head, throw their musk at your feet
In the apricot dusk. But the house has gone.

Harvest

You are cross. Since you have my acid tongue
Like early apples with their white pips,

You are thought unkind at school.
A mealy softness, such as slips

From foreign peel, might serve you well.
For a time, a time. But soon

Lit by snow, the orchards stand.
Strange and sharp the steady moon.

Cycles

Would I go back? The childhood bike
Was secondhand, painted thick blue.
Yet scratch the hedge, dull black showed through.
I rattled blank lanes where I liked.
I had a college bike, caught hard
In its top gear, when I met you.
Uphill, I fought for every yard.

When I first worked, roads gave more space.
I steered cheap bikes through tall streets, full
Of selfish hopes, the first air cool.
Some came, some went. Sun scorched my face.
I whirred electric windows down.
Caught in the traffic's throb and pull
I drove my daughter into town.

This bike is new. It shines and purrs.
I shake, but can still pedal, swoop
From our workshop's door in crazy loops
Behind old roofs. My fine gears whirr,
I set off home. Lit trees storm past,
Late rain holds off, stiff knees hold out.
Oh never have I gone so fast.

Autumn Street

There are three houses in this road
In which a child should have been born.
The first was caught upon a screen.
It floated in the womb's pool, dead.

Then, in a cool September week,
A boy was born with his lip split.
It has been sewn, to leave it neat.
I do not know how he will speak.

The third, a son, was born so soon
He weighs less than a loaf of bread.
His skull's blue vein-maps tick and spread,
A fledgling's head the wind blew down.

Thistles and dandelions, yet green,
Cloud the late sky with glistening seed
At which we stare, in empty need
Upon blue air, its waste and sheen.

A. Pennington

Andrew, plump and young, perched on my sofa
In his unfashionable black overcoat
Plotted, guffawed, the keen young councillor.
'I only hope I live to see the day
When we have made that wretched grammar school
A comprehensive school for Hester's Way.'

Who was Hester, once? I doubt if Andrew
Could have told you that. The peeling towers
Might have scared her, bare parks where needles blew.
He bounced along her ground. Scuffed overcoat
Flapped. He fought for buses, surgeries.
Neighbours brought forms, grief; tea. He earned each vote.

I grew busy. I did less. Andrew, I know,
Grew busier, did more. I saw his name
Blur on each pamphlet like a light through snow.
And how he beamed, and how the May crowd roared
When his friend was named MP. One January
A man came walking with a foreign sword

A man who had lost job and house and mind.
Trapped in the small bare office where they worked
His friend, the tall MP, had a slashed hand.
Andrew ran out for help, rushed back inside.
Called from the windswept, ordinary street,
A stranger took him in his arms. He died.

My tall slim daughter, on the sofa still,
Stares wearily at me. 'It can't be done;
They never will close down the grammar school.'
'Did Andrew ever start with "can't"?' I say:
A small man, whom a town will not forget,
A man who always knew that we are they.

Virtue

Virtue on a bicycle
Pants beneath the sun.
Ease jumps lightly in her car
Then flicks the radio on.

Virtue, halfway up the hill
Sees the storm clouds glare.
Ease waves to her, sailing by.
She scrapes back her soaked hair.

Ease, with her fine bones, took her love.
She has no tears to cry.
The bicycle skims down the hill.
Her face is kissed by sky.

Curriculum

Does anyone learn science at school?
Someone must. We would have no
Castors, phones or superglue.
For most of us, science taught a smell

Of dark and chipped laboratories
In which spilt acid spat from sinks.
Beakers from which you dared not drink,
The chalked equations' mysteries.

The bunsen burners' wavering
Gave light to this low-ceilinged place
Taught me one fact. I stared, when told,
At the heart of the flame's hissing
Past gold heat. Through the windless space
Blue equalled silent, perfect cold.

Set

Stand at the high yard's edge tonight.
Six planets wait you in twilight.

Mercury's low, the frail child
Who sees his screaming friends run wild.

Mars hangs dull red, the frowning one.
Saturn whirls on, her hair's clouds down.

Jupiter climbs old stars' glitter –
Guest who nods at someone better.

White fire is Venus, steady, sure.
Your eyes burn to her from the door.

Where is the sixth? Its blood is red.
Its tides break softly in your head.

What You See

It is so cold a night
The helicopter's sides
Above unseen rail lines
Flash silver flanks, not white.

How skilfully it hangs
Upon the black loud air.
The searchlight pours down where
We think, a burglar runs.

It is so simple. So,
How great, the shock next day.
On steel the dead man lay,
Whose name we never know.

Joggers

You could easily run them down.
Some are slippery in yellow, as fish
Slice the dark's waters. Others strip down
To a flicker of cloth, a wish

To pound still further. Some are jowled,
Mottled by age. Some race, so young
You scarcely remember that energy
A trap will shiver, sprung.

Although I can picture the tendon's tear
Though I feel in my own knees the grind of worn bone
I am stirred and moved by their flight to air
From the choke of the traffic, the silence of stone.

After the Rats

I married the piper.
It was not brave.
He could make dull stones dance,
The dead spin on their graves.

Does he swoop me to sleep?
Do I float through my days
As fish slip unmoving
Through blue and green haze?

Do I starve on the streets?
Or repent of my sin,
Break my fist on neat doors
Crying 'Let me back in'?

None of this. I survive,
My four children stretch tall;
But the piper grows grey
And my pension is small.

We do not wake all day,
Sleep the whole night.
I sing on frost's doorstep.
My voice thins to light.

The Town Gulls

Hawkers, squawkers, yappers, why
Have they left the pebbles' wide
Snarl of sea for roofs' dry height,
Trawlers for the dustmen's cart?

Warmth is simpler. One great gull
Drops below the dusk winds' pull,
Soot-backed on the chimney's cowl
Spreads his wings on hot draughts' swell.

One crashed fledgling fell, landlocked,
In a backyard. Walls loomed, blocked
Veering flight. It crumpled, flopped,
Spent a loud night in a box,

Ushered out, on the pavement,
Shrieked. Its diving parents set
Lurching runs up, till it met
Air, our truest element,

Circled, wings smudged with clinker,
As rain clouds smouldered higher
She left wet soil beneath her,
Swept wind's light, air and fire.

Counting

Once money flowed round us like friends,
Salaries, gifts, dividends.
A gurgle. The long party ends,

Each bank account dry as a throat,
Each rustle of bills a new note,
Alarm, as the rabbit meets stoat.

Wide headlights sweep on. Out of glare,
The bruises fade. Time to repair,
To count up loose change on the stair,

To queue in Co-ops with quiet old men,
Hoard slips for razor blades, find them
Flashed cheap, in corner shops you spurned.

It is a losing game, you feel,
With money lost which oiled the wheel
(At each slow crank the rust cogs squeal).

One post, a sudden legacy
Might cast this time to memory
A grey-lit dusk slid under sea,

When days of drudging wore your mind,
When walking's warm wind blew, unsigned,
When neighbours spoke, when you were kind.

R. ficaria

I study celandines.
Ranunculus
floods the borders
lifts to us

its mops of brazen gold,
the common sun.
The catalogues silt.
It is only one

of fifty, a hundred,
white, bronze, blue
to their well-bred tips.
I buy a few.

Entranced by doubles,
by rarity
of marbled leaf
I read late, see

marvellous hybrids
fill my grasp.
In dark, the experts
munch, dig, rasp.

Morning in the Shop

At seven-ten he bought his cake, he says,
He strolled back home then found his neighbour dead.
It is half-past eight now. He asks for cigarettes.

He lay wedged against the door. They had to break the glass.
'I did hear that,' a woman says. 'I wondered what it was.
Not a good way to go.' 'I've not stopped shaking yet.

I went down to his sister's. We had a cup of tea.'
He is old; and worn to bone. He does not look at me.
They walk across the concrete where the garages have been.

The morning haze breathes slowly in the cool September air.
Blue clouding from his cigarette fades hot and tender there.
It is a day as beautiful as any he has seen.

Looking Through

I read newspapers, endlessly,
when I should be doing
so many things. The actresses are best
in the obituaries: their tiny bones,
their triple marriages. How often they end up
With a dog, upon a ranch, alone.

What does this tell me, about women,
even about dogs? Nothing.
It is the soul
Which loves to look at mountains, in clear air.

Behind Lansdown Crescent

It is not rain. The forecast says so.
The sky is crisp and the birch tree rustles
By the dark wall, wind's shiver, not rain.

What is this which brushes my eyelid?
Stars of coolness light my face.
In dry back lanes, it is not rain,
A leaf, a tear, a smudge of grace.

Severe Weather Warning

The walls are firm. The central heating hums,
Cars wait; but I am a slave to weather.
I sit in clouded light. The forecast comes,
The horse is miles away, on the harsh hills.
Storms will strike us; as the sodden leather
Slips from my fingers, as the branch-fall kills

The young girl in her soft-topped car. At home
My dearest projects wait for kinder air.
New bulbs, adrift on Latin names like foam,
Float in their box. They should be anchored in
The tideless ground: dark arums, sleek as hair
Under hoods. Earth lies too wet for trampling.

Others are free, detached. They watch their screens,
They drive to drinks with friends. I watch the sky,
Its maddening dazzle and its lemon streams
Of sun through rain's dark tails. By the poor school
Soaked starlings wheel from oaks. They scatter high.
I live in the wind's thrust, by the sun's rule.

But why? I left the country. Join the town.
The soil beneath the drive tugs at my heel.
This is like trusting luck, whirled high, cast down.
It is. But weather has a fierce ghost.
Its wet black wing has touched my face. I feel
It breathe, stretch, wake, before quick cars and toast.

The Sunday Outing

Is someone crying? No, it is the train
Whispering the rails, chuntering its brakes.
I travel to my old school friend again.
Rain wrinkles on the Midland fields in lakes.

I knew of the divorce; not that her husband
Clamped hose to the exhaust. He would not live.
Frantic, she hunted down the darkening lanes.
He phoned. The hose was worn. He did survive.

Her son, the cheerful child, dropped out of school,
Fuchsias storm her fence. I go, still trying
To swim through dates. Girls leave; my empty coach
Rattles to the station. I am crying.

Empires

The isles' last horse is dead.
Its legs stretch stiff and straight.
The winds which beat its head

Blew all bees out to sea.
Ship ponies in. Or wait
The wind's first breath of honey.

At Manor Farm

Tom Pickernell, Mr Thomas
To the rough lads on the course
Sprints through his father's orchard
To check his favourite horse,

Runs hands along cool tendons,
Trots past gold ghosts of pear.
His father's cider apples
Float red moons on first air.

Still sweated from the gallop
He bites on choicest fruit,
His hunter chomps the windfalls
Bruised sweet amongst the roots.

A lord dreams that his racehorse,
His tiny horse, the Lamb,
Loses, then wins the National.
'Tom Pickernell's your man,'

Whispers the dream, half-sourly,
As kiss of cider breath.
Tom Pickernell bursts through the mud.
The Lamb's sides heave like death

But stagger them to history.
Tom wins the race twice more.
His father dies. Falls smash his head.
His credit is withdrawn.

He mortgages, sells half the farm,
Morosely, shuts the door.
Dusk swallows up his cider trees.
Tom Pickernell downs one more.

Tom Pickernell dies in Birmingham,
His whip hand cracks the glass.
The Lamb lifts sweetly to the last.
Ripe apples heap the grass.

The Lincolnshire Accent

It is a voice even in men
Turned hesitant
A child who now has lost the note
His mother sent.
It starts in warmth but then the vowels
Begin to blur,
Give words no end. A lamb's wide cries
Crumble to air.
My uncle's voice, my grandfather's,
Sift quiet through death.
A Scunthorpe girl speaks in the news.
I hold my breath.

'Tell me again, more slowly.
I did not understand.'
'The young king, fresh from marriage,
Rode to a neighbour's land.
He changed shape with the other
Yet kept his own clear mind.'
'But why?' 'They thought (as you may)
To take what they could find.

There was a girl – now listen –
As bright, as fierce as air.
He courted her in his friend's shape,
His eyes looked through her there.
She stretched out her strong hand to him
But when he bedded her
He laid a sword with damasked edge
Between them, sharp and bare.'

'So did they reach across the blade
To breast or thigh's curve?' 'No.
Eight days they spent together,
Eight deep nights, sleeping so.
When they rode from her country
The false mind took the true,
A husband with familiar face
But not the man she knew.'

'How can this end?' 'Too quickly:
She plotted, so he died.
She held no thought for his kind wife
Who huddled, small, and cried.
She left her sleeping husband
Whose bed sank soft and wide
Stabbed her heart with the king's sword,
Then lay down by his side.'

'This is an old, bad story
Whose truth cannot be known,
A knot now pulled too tightly,
The hand which tied it gone.
How can I understand it
Whose pain is not my own?'
'The blade you lay beneath your sheets
Will cut you to the bone.'

Moonlight

The favourite; not for beauty
Though tabbies now are rare
Or great sweetness of nature
But being there

Curled on the stones for gardening
On Sunday, on the bed
Stealing the milk's last whisker.
The runt, he fed

Frantically ever after.
He swayed across the room
Until the face grew lean as lynx
The hips a hill of bone.

A quiet cat from the country
Born in a haystack's scent
We rescued him from drowning.
But life is only lent.

Though other cats crowd after
More beautiful, more sweet,
He waits at my eye's corner
The shadow at my feet.

Customer

You do not know why I cried last night
Why the last sandwich sailed into the hedge.
You did not see the cat with smudged grey ruff
Freeze by my tyres, spring lightly to the edge.

You do not know my parents' Christian names,
My daughter's voice, or where I went to school
Nor tell from my too-careful ironed-out tone
Who I once loved; and who I think a fool.

I come in twice a week to pick through bread
Choose cabbages, complain about the flu
Beg a stout box and melt into the rain
And so you think you know me. And you do.

Cold April

The buzzards grow tiny. They mew,
A white sound, with no pity.
With buckled wings they plunge
The storeys of air's city.

Wings' edges open fingers.
At idle height they glide.
Snow's sudden light enthrals
Their ruffled underside.

Why three? I cannot see
Their pairing, pain or kin,
Indifferent as the clouds' tails
They sweep; they circle in,

Low trees duck to their landing.
They need heath, gorse and broom.
World is too small for them. Tall men
Stoop, to a narrow room.

Livestock

Those bloody sheep! So my father called them.
For unless the flock was provisioned well
His father uprooted to one more farm.
Yet I always liked them; the hand-reared lambs
With collars and leads, who skinned my knuckles
On the orchard tree; the blank mild dams

Whom I could not herd; for sheep are stubborn,
Nor could I count, as they milled round the troughs.
But still, I look for the breeds; the Roman
White face of the Suffolk; the huge Romney;
The tough mountain Mules. My practised throat bleats,
The white head jerks up. It calls back to me.

The old farmer rings, who used to tell me
His name and his home-place, trick of a lord.
His hands, huge red bundles, restore bikes. Today
'I've no livestock left,' he says. 'Just dead stock.'
(It was Foot and Mouth.) 'They just took them away.'

On his empty farm, in the chilly shed
He has rigged up a vat. My husband comes.
'You'll find exhaust pipes are always cratered.
The minimum temperature? I don't know.
We don't do copper. I'll look it up… sixty?
A pig lamp? Maybe. Your current's too low.'

They hunch at each end with their manuals.
I never eat meat, have no more to do.
Through the workshop's door, the dull rain sizzles
Which the virus loves. The trucks hit the deep
Pocks in the lane. The small carcasses throb,
Why do I still cry for these bloody sheep?

Pegglesworth

The field's a blonde sea. The sheep, white whales,
Graze down the deeps. The pony, a ship,
Sways through the swells where they whisk their strong tails.

Are these sheep for slaughter? Are all poems lies?
No sea breathes pale pollen, or maddens with flies.

Up

Christmas, midnight. Though nearly fifty
You should hurry to bed.
You will drift tomorrow from hot afternoon,
Wake, dusk's ache in your head.

But you hear night stretch above your window,
The stars lick tongues of cold.
You place the shining cards on one shelf,
Silver, silver, gold to gold.

Star Notes: November

The Leonids, the paper said
Would swarm like bees above our heads
The last great meteor shower to see
This dark side of the century.

Frost–gripped, we huddled once to find
Them streak above the washing line.
Low garages, small ash trees shrank
Beneath the black seas that they drank.

The comet's frozen dirty tail
Burned for us. But the weak stars fail.
Tonight the soft cloud wraps hills round.
A wet grey fog weeps on the ground.

Preoccupied, I work on late
Forget all skies; but early, wake,
Scramble on boots and dressing gown.
A blue sky rushes over, blown

Clear as a bird's egg, hollow moon
Hangs, past the ashes' budded tower,
Hot silver smudge, the meteor
Flashes its miles. In burning dive
Low, incandescent, I count five

Until the last is lapped by cloud.
Elbows grow chill, an engine loud,
Then morning's crash. The milkman's race
Drops six white bottles in our space.

Travelled

In Turkey, young and thoughtless
We never came to Troy.
What damage did we do there?
What happened to the boy

Whose family we wrote to?
Was he thrown into jail?
The grass was glowing by the sea
Troy was an empty tale.

Sharp waves flood through my head now
Whose salt has parched my joy.
My child is lost in sharp grass.
I touch the walls of Troy.

The North Room

I have seen unhappiness, who stood
In a high Oxford room, beside my bed.
The room was narrow. I think she was a maid.
She certainly was dead.

It was that time of darkness, when you wake
Tunnelled from morning, half-choked by despair.
There was no lace, or whispered words to take:
A thickening of the air

Which brushed against the lips, caught in the throat,
Cleared, with the buzzing of a midnight fly.
Next term I had the front room. It shone west.
I swung the bed to sky.

A Brief History

O in the eighteenth century
When opera was reborn
No end was ever tragic
No heart was ever torn

Apollo could not mend in song.
I find such warm light hard.
I think that Anastasia fell.
But howling in the yard

Their English spaniel stayed, half-starved.
Its name survived too. Joy.
What last charge rode Prince Rupert down?
His poodle's name was Boy.

Did it bounce past the Civil War?
The first dog shot through space
Has a soft name, which starts with L.
It died in that chill race.

I start to whistle quietly
A low song out of tune.
The Russian dog, then Joy and Boy
Grave as this autumn's moon

Speak, as though I understood.
(They know I have no choice.)
'This music tells the end of time.
It needs no human voice.'

Hatherley Lane School
1878–2001

Prologue

Bell's glint, brick, oak, me. School.
Where did those jackdaws come from
with their black and tumbling wings?

The children? Most sang loud.
Irene, who never could
do sums, was let to run for bread and cheese,

the master's lunch,
up lanes, the tree-hung bridge.
Then children marched away,

lost in a new road's roar,
found lower rooms. I soon lost count
of Irene, whistling by, her head ruffed grey.

I stood a store
my green bell silent. Was it then
the jackdaws tickled through my gable stones?

Papers rustle. I hear 'Sold'.
Though I am old, I am no fool.
I shall be dust, join all lost things.

What can my going give to you?
You built, you died. You grew no wings.

Campaign

The children of the school I work to save,
Victoria's children, dead a life ago,
come to me in the dawn. 'No, go away,'
I say, 'I do not like you.

I would not slave to starch your pinafores,
and, from the country too, I know you killed
with careless hunger, frogs, soft-throated birds.
Go back into the marsh

whose oozing tracks you thread. What did you do
in class? You sang, you bawled.
The school's a shell
we fill with our own echoes – Do not cry.

Look, here is the dirt road, the fancy house
with locked iron gates, then Mrs Willis' shop.
Here is a penny with a rubbed Queen's head.'

But no, they stand and frown; then toss their heads
like ponies. They are thick and hurt and strong.
They never wanted school. They choose the path
where the spring bubbles, where the grass soars long.

Mrs Hyde Clark

I knew her house with its wide eaves
Where martins flashed into the sun.
When it came down, I did not grieve,
I did not know all she had done,
Brought children in from the first school,
Into her own room, so the sun

Could flood across the lines they ruled,
Then smudged. They heard men hammering
The roof's oak ship for their new school,
Whose bell rocked by the railway,
Where she sent oranges, her clock,
As marsh and orchards stretched away.

Hot steel of rails rang, and struck
Into a time that they would know
Crowded with roofs, more free from luck
And scarlet fever, where we know
Our solid school, beneath its tower,
May be torn down for bungalows.

The school's logs tell us every hymn
Those children sang. I listen hard
As blue bricks shine. Their grandchildren,
Now grandmothers, scrawl 'Save our School!'
An old voice crackles, down the phone,
'A buyer! The Evangelicals!'

Tall pear trees in cool grass are gone.
In our close houses' anxious peace
We do not want thin walls to drone
Loud hymns, black prayers. I am the cause,
I worked for this. I close my eyes.
Her voice sings on. God, it grows worse.

'Discos – youth clubs –' A light spins free.
Tough as old bricks, rehoused by Heaven,
Mrs Hyde Clark winks down at me.

Architect

John Middleton, architect, wrote on these plans
The first month of frost; the name of this town
Where his sharp pen sliced immaculate joists
For the high hall roof cranes may wrench down.

Were his quick hands thin, or veined with blue?
Were they weighed by rings, which chilled the cheek?
He came to retire, as the journalists knew.
His Clarence Street office opened that week.

I gaze at his churches; street after street
Sheer, shadowed walls rise; his striped arches try
Clouded blues, Forest stone. But where are the spires?
The town's cash was meagre. He wanted the sky.

High Church or Low Church, he worked for them all,
Then to fever wards! His pen never stopped.
By the Ladies' College, I squint through haze
At the tall unnecessary tower he topped

With sunned red tiles. Carved tangles of leaf
Turn a grate to riot. My warmed thoughts feel
Another summer – Italy?
A woman's laughter. Not Miss Beale.

I could have shown you John Middleton's dreams,
The high stone cave of a house where he spent
Short evenings with gargoyles, gilt's glint, tiles
Whose plasterers sailed from the Continent.

His son loved the Gothic, then sold on the firm.
What drugs feed a dead dream? Close to his time
John Middleton sketched out a small, church school
Without a fee, or one smudged line.

He drew red roof-tiles, pierced to sky.
He set stout brick in herringbone.
He gave each gable one black flower
And for its sill, blue Forest stone.

But the school may fall. For his own house crashed,
Gilt to plain dust, lost to pension one man's
Old age. Can our work save anything good?
We drain our coffee. We pick up his plans.

The Pillbox

The Gunny was a concrete block
Which stood above a railway line
Nodded and fretted under trees
In a school playground, out of town.

The children pushed inside its door
Poked fingers through its slatted wall,
'Bang!' Then later? Sixty, neat,
They laugh and flush; do not tell all.

They were the children of the peace
Who lived in prefabs by the flat
Fields with ridge and furrows' shade
Where water rats plopped large as cats.

They bought cool fridges and warm cars
But woke to see the long fields gone,
Wrote awkward letters to save trees.
The Gunny, in its shade, stayed on

Above rails' glint, where day and night
The frightened boys had rattled by.
Bomb craters flashed with newts; were drained.
Large houses marched. 'But is the Gunny

Still there?' they asked me, hopefully.
'Oh yes!' I cried; till driving by
Too fast, my shopping heaped, I saw
The broken white blocks piled up high.

Is the tree next? Why should we care
If we sleep safely in new beds?
The Gunny, lost to the dry ground
Joins rubble in our hearts and heads.

Owners

After the meeting she comes to me.
I have not won. I have merely held
The bulldozers back for a few more weeks
Till the belltower falls and the trees are felled.

But the crowd, who do not understand, are smiling.
I smile too; then I see her stand
Gaunt and dark, in a long flowered dress.
Her bony fingers grip my hand.

'Thank you,' I murmur. 'I don't think we've met?
I'm sorry,' I probe. 'I don't know your name.'
She springs back from me like a cat.
She lifts her head, past fear or blame.

'I am the owner of the school.
Nobody mentioned *my* name,' she spits
Then turns on her heel. How did the crowd take her?
I stand, by laughter; heat; cherry-pits.

Yes, I have heard of her. She is ill,
Bones crowd her face. I carry on.
'Thank you,' I say to the strangers. 'Thank you.'
I watch the door where I have gone.

Out of the Picture

Tossed by wet April, we stood on the bridge.
A pupil's granddaughter sucked milk in her shawl.
The photographer cried, 'Look sad for the school!'
We shivered. We frowned. His light froze us all.

The school stood still in a summer's rain.
The planning posters came and went.
He applied. We objected. They voted him down.
The heat grew fierce. The jackdaws spent

Long mornings on the cool ridge tiles
Till blue day lengthened and they flew.
The day the men arrived with cranes
One whispered past my face like snow.

'Stand by the gate,' the photographer said.
'I can get the holes in the roof from there.
Can't you blockade the street where he lives?'
The roof's oak bones rose clean to air.

We measure our low trees for new, wooden roosts.
But the jackdaws sweep over, their stone gables gone.
I fly round the corner. Great diggers crouch there.
High nests crowd the beams; find cold wind. I drive on.

The Day Before

Then in the end I walked alone
To the garden's fence, and saw the school.
The elders in the way were gone.

The belltower glinted in the sun.
The stripped roof by the railway line
Lay shadowed, but the west wall shone

With one great window, as the space
In its last tree blew fresh and strong.
I stared upon it as a face

Whose youth defied the moments' rule.
I squinted through the sun and saw
For the first time, the country school

Without its tarmac, cars or wires,
Where children filed through its low door.
I smelt the smoke of its lost fires,

Their wet wool coats. What had I seen?
It had escaped from us at last.
It ended as it once had been.

Invitation to an Entertainment

It is March, 1900. The windy sky
Up Hatherley Lane is not neon but green.
In the schoolroom, the Night School concert starts.
They cough. Milly yawns, surveys the scene.

Mr Edward Easterfield takes the Chair,
BA; half-bald. She stares instead
At the boy at the front, with soft dark hair.
She longs for her supper-plate's warm, cracked bread.

The chair and the corset dig in her back.
Mr Edward Easterfield's smile is grim.
The branches stir in the restless dark.
What can she do? 'Let us start with a hymn.'

She does not know how fat she will grow,
That her first son's father will be dead
How the cars will roar, how the school will fall.
The boy smiles back. She cocks her head.

The piano peals. She scrapes her chair,
Her best white blouse puffs up like wings.
The school sails on, to our reckless dark.
Milly opens her throat and sings.

Late Again

Time (I say quickly) is giving me grief.
Computers nibble it. Sleep devours it.
I have lost the tree in the clutter of leaf.

Time will bring me the lighter evenings,
The sheath of the tulip, the call from a friend.
Time will weigh me, mock me, dismay me.
Time is the clocks' dream. Time will end.